Original title:

Xenon Flickers Above the Dragon Cup

Author: Sara Säde

ISBN HARDBACK: 978-1-80563-058-6

ISBN PAPERBACK: 978-1-80564-579-5

Luminous Threads Woven from Fiery Dreams

In twilight's grasp, where shadows blend,
A tapestry of hopes we send.
With each bright thread, a story spun,
Illuminated by a setting sun.

The stars above in silence gleam,
Guiding us through night's gentle beam.
With every flicker, a wish ignites,
In the heart's embers, a dance of lights.

In realms of magic, we dare to soar,
On fiery dreams, forevermore.
Woven tightly, our fates entwine,
In this realm, the stars align.

Through whispers soft, a secret shared,
In dreams, our spirits unprepared.
With laughter bright and love's sweet grace,
We journey onward, face to face.

So let us weave our tales anew,
With threads of gold and skies so blue.
For in this dance of light and shade,
Our luminous paths will never fade.

Flickering Flames Beneath Celestial Guardians

Beneath the stars, a flicker glows,
As ancient tales in stillness flow.
Guardians watch with watchful eyes,
As dreams take flight and softly rise.

The flames that dance in gentle air,
Whisper secrets beyond compare.
With every spark, a hope reborn,
In the embrace of night's adorn.

Celestial light, a guiding hand,
As stardust gathers on the land.
Each flicker sings a silent song,
A melody of right and wrong.

In shadows deep, the warmth we find,
Connection forged, our hearts aligned.
Beneath the sky, so vast and wide,
In flickering flames, our dreams abide.

Together we shall brave the night,
With spirits bold, our hearts alight.
For in this realm where fates entwine,
Beneath celestial guardians, we shine.

Aether's Whisper Through the Arcane

In the aether, soft whispers call,
Echoing through the ancient hall.
Secrets wrapped in silken haze,
A dance of magic, an endless maze.

With every breath, the arcane sighs,
A symphony of hidden skies.
In shadows deep, the spirits roam,
In woven fate, we find our home.

Threads of magic, spun with care,
Float lightly on the midnight air.
In twilight's glow, our hearts entwine,
With each soft word, a spark divine.

Through twilight woods and starry streams,
We weave together our flickering dreams.
In the hush of night, the world awakes,
With gentle magic, the heart remakes.

So listen close to the night's embrace,
And find the magic in every space.
For aether's whispers, sweet and rare,
Will guide us forth, beyond despair.

Hereditary Embers Amidst High Spirits

Embers flicker in the dark,
A legacy, a vibrant spark.
Within our veins, the warmth remains,
Through highs and lows, we share the gains.

High spirits lift us in their dance,
To ancient songs, we take our chance.
With every heartbeat, a story told,
In whispers soft, the brave and bold.

Our roots run deep like oak and vine,
Connected through the sands of time.
In unity, we face the night,
Hereditary embers, burning bright.

Through trials faced and battles won,
Our family shines, a blazing sun.
In every glance, our ancestors smile,
Together we journey, mile by mile.

So let the embers glow and shine,
In every soul, a thread divine.
With high spirits, hand in hand we roam,
In this vast world, we have our home.

A Dance Beneath the Glint of Stars

In moonlit clear, the shadows sway,
With whispers soft, they dance and play.
Beneath the vast, embracing night,
A tapestry of dreams takes flight.

The twinkling gems, they beckon near,
In every glimmer, hope and fear.
A waltz of souls, so light and free,
In harmony, we breathe and see.

The breeze carries tales, both lost and found,
In every heartbeat, secrets sound.
With stars aligned, the world does pause,
A universe, where love is cause.

As dawn approaches, lights will fade,
Yet in this night, our hearts were laid.
So step with me, into the glow,
A dance of shadows, a soft echo.

Ethereal Light in the Keeper's Sanctuary

Within the walls of ancient stone,
A keeper waits, so not alone.
With gentleness, the light unfolds,
In secrets kept, in stories told.

Ethereal glow, so soft, so bright,
Guiding lost souls through the night.
Each flicker holds a sacred past,
In whispered winds that dance so fast.

The air is thick with ageless lore,
Where dreams once soared, and spirits soar.
A sanctuary forged in grace,
Where every heart finds its place.

Time stops still for those who seek,
In this abode where souls shall speak.
With every breath, the light does sing,
Awakening, a new beginning.

Glimmers of Glory in the Dragon's Nest

In lofty heights where legends dwell,
A nest of flames, where stories swell.
With scales that shimmer, eyes that gleam,
A guardian fierce of a timeless dream.

Glimmers bright in the twilight sky,
As echoes of ancients drift and sigh.
Each feathered flame, a tale retold,
Of valor found and treasures bold.

Amongst the stars, the dragons soar,
With thunderous roars, they long for more.
In every heartbeat, courage flies,
In deep, wild realms, where magic lies.

From ashes rise, the phoenix sings,
In a world where hope forever clings.
Glimmers of glory, fierce and bright,
In the dragon's nest, we find our light.

Enigmatic Glow on the Edge of Chaos

On chaos' brink, where shadows wane,
An enigmatic glow breaks the chain.
With threads of fate that intertwine,
A dance of dangers, bold, divine.

In whispered winds, the ancients plot,
A world unspooled, a tangled knot.
Yet in the murk, a lantern's gleam,
A flicker caught within the dream.

The stars align in cryptic signs,
In cosmic fields where destiny shines.
Through trials faced, each heart must fight,
To carve a path into the light.

Though chaos reigns, the heart stays true,
In every struggle, strength anew.
We find our way through dark and storm,
An enigmatic glow keeps us warm.

Veils of Light Upon a Scaled Goblet

In shadows cast by flickering flames,
A goblet gleams with ancient names.
Veils of light dance in the night,
Whispers lost in the shimmering bright.

Scales adorned with stories untold,
Echoes of magic, brave and bold.
Each sip a journey through time and space,
Where dreams awaken, and fears erase.

Within its depths, the stars align,
A secret world dwarfed by design.
With every pulse, the goblet sings,
Of forgotten realms and fateful things.

The flicker turns to a radiant glow,
As veils of wisdom ebb and flow.
In stillness held, the moment breathes,
A tapestry woven in silver leaves.

So raise the cup, let your heart recite,
The verses born of starlit night.
For in this goblet, legends entwine,
Forever marked by the hand of time.

Whispers of Radiance in the Dragon's Keep

Within the walls of stone and flame,
A dragon guards its sacred claim.
Whispers floating on the breeze,
Radiance flickers with effortless ease.

In twilight's embrace, the lanterns sway,
casting shadows where dragons play.
Stories woven through sands of gold,
In every heart, the legends told.

From treasure bright to the darkest depths,
Echoes linger with every step.
In the keeper's eye, a spark of light,
Guiding seekers through endless night.

Chants of old dance through the air,
Brimming with magic, rare and fair.
Crimson hues and emerald scales,
Trust the whispers in wondrous tales.

Embrace the warmth of the dragon's might,
For therein lies the path to light.
In the keep where shadows loom,
Radiance flourishes, dispelling gloom.

Celestial Sparks Above the Enchanted Cup

Above the cup, the cosmos sprawls,
Celestial sparks in silken thralls.
They twinkle like dreams yet to unfold,
In the glow of magic, both shy and bold.

Layers of stardust drape the night,
As wishes scatter in the soft twilight.
The enchanted cup holds secrets deep,
In its embrace, even silence speaks.

Moments captured in shimmering hues,
A canvas where the heart will choose.
As each spark dances in the air,
Whispers rise with the vibrant flare.

So sip from the cup, let the dreams ignite,
Feel the warmth of the stars in flight.
Celestial wonders, vast and free,
Transform the ordinary to magic's decree.

In each sip, a journey awaits,
Beyond the realms, through hidden gates.
Carry the light, hold it near,
For the enchanted cup dispels all fear.

Reflections of the Obsidian Beast

In shadows dark, the beast resides,
Within its gaze, the secret hides.
Reflections whisper of ancient lore,
Echoes dance on the cavern floor.

Obsidian scales, like twilight's veil,
Shimmer and glisten, a haunting tale.
In stillness, time begins to wane,
As the beast awakens to break the chain.

Eyes like stars, piercing and bright,
Unfurling stories of courage and light.
Its heart beats with the rhythm of night,
A guardian fierce, yet gentle in flight.

Legends tread softly on dragonwind,
Where shadows linger, hope rescinds.
Through cracks of time, the echoes flow,
Reflections of power in the darkened glow.

Embrace the fear, let it inspire,
For within the beast lies burning fire.
In every ripple of the obsidian sheen,
A world awaits, serene yet unseen.

Celestial Glow Within the Fabled Keep

In the heart of the ancient stone,
Where whispers of magic softly moan,
Glimmers of starlight gently weave,
A tapestry of dreams to believe.

Chandeliers of moonlight dance in glee,
Casting shadows where the lost wander free,
Fables echo through corridors wide,
As secrets of time in silence abide.

A guardian's ghost, with eyes aglow,
Guides the seekers where the wonders flow,
Through hallowed halls where legends reside,
In the embrace of enchantment, they bide.

Frosted whispers upon the chill air,
Tellers of tales beyond compare,
With each step taken on storied ground,
Magic and history intertwine around.

The keep stands tall, a sentinel bright,
Cradling the eve, cradling the night,
While celestial tides in stillness sweep,
In the fabled glow, the world falls asleep.

Wyrmkin Shimmers Across the Horizon

Across the sky, where dreams take flight,
Wyrmkin glimmers in the waning light,
Scales like embers in the azure blue,
A dance of shadows, a majestic view.

They spiral high on wings so vast,
Carving tales of the shivering past,
With roars that echo through valleys deep,
Awakening legends from eternal sleep.

In twilight's grasp, they weave a song,
A harmony where lost souls belong,
Each note a spark in the evening's glow,
A celestial promise with each wind's flow.

Beneath the stars, they sweep and soar,
Guardians of skies, of ancient lore,
As night drapes softly, their silhouettes play,
Wyrmkin shimmer in the dimming day.

With hearts aglow in the dusk's embrace,
They carry the dreams of an hidden place,
Where magic flows like the rivers wide,
And all our hopes on the wings abide.

A Luminous Watch Above the Ancient Forge

In the heart of the mountain, flames arise,
Forging the steel beneath open skies,
Anvil and hammer in rhythmic grace,
Crafting the future in this sacred space.

Above the forge, stars twinkle bright,
A celestial watch over the fiery sight,
Their light spills down in shimmering streams,
Igniting the night with the power of dreams.

With sparks that dance like fireflies bold,
Tales of creation silently unfold,
Each strike a testament, each flame a song,
In the ancient forge where memories throng.

The shadows of giants echo their craft,
Legends of old in each fiery draft,
As the forge breathes magic through iron veins,
Etching on time what forever remains.

In luminous silence, the stars conspire,
To guide the hands that shape and inspire,
For in this warmth, the world shapes anew,
Forged in the blaze, where dreams come true.

Twilight's Embrace Over Mythic Fire

When twilight falls, the colors entwine,
A symphony played, both tender and fine,
Mythic fire flickers, casting its glow,
A glowing reminder of tales we know.

In the dance of embers, stories arise,
Whispers of heroes beneath evening skies,
The warmth of the flame wraps souls in delight,
Carrying memories through the soft night.

Creatures of twilight gather in lore,
Each shadow a tale, each flicker a score,
As night deepens over the enchanted grove,
In the heart of the flames, the world learns to move.

Embrace the moment, the flickers divine,
For magic entwines in the borders of time,
Within each heartbeat, each whispered name,
The fire remembers, the night lights the flame.

So sit by the blaze, let your spirit ignite,
In twilight's embrace, the wonders take flight,
For mythic fire lives in the pulse of the hour,
A testament to dreams, a potent power.

Radiant Dreams in the Dragon's Keep

In the darkened halls where shadows creep,
A siren's song, and secrets seep.
Glimmers of gold in a fire's arc,
Breath of magic ignites the spark.

Guarded whispers of ages past,
Echoes of glory, shadows cast.
Dragon's breath in a misty shroud,
Dreams entwined with a billowy cloud.

Wings spread wide in a graceful leap,
As night enfolds the world in sleep.
Glory awaits in the keeper's thrall,
Radiant dreams in realms of all.

Crimson scales in the moon's cool light,
Adventures wait beyond the night.
With every heartbeat, the magic swells,
In the dragon's keep, where mystery dwells.

Glimmers of Mystique Over Ancient Chalices

In silence deep, a chalice gleams,
With secrets whispered in silver streams.
Ancient tales within its curves,
Echoing magic the heart preserves.

Glimmers of mystique in moonlit flow,
With eyes like stars, they ebb and glow.
Woven spells in the midnight air,
Conjuring wonders beyond compare.

From vine to vine, the stories weave,
Gifting us moments that we believe.
Timeless dances on twilight's brink,
Unlock the heart, invite the ink.

Chalices raised to the velvet sky,
Carrying dreams that never die.
In the shadows, true magic stirs,
With whispers soft, the universe purrs.

Twilight's Dance with Glowing Relics

In twilight's embrace, the relics glow,
Each dance a story, each heart a flow.
Cloaked in shadows, mystery waits,
Infinite wonders and enchanted fates.

With every step, the night unfolds,
Ancient magic in the air re-holds.
Whispers of long-lost, timeless sights,
Shimmering softly under starry nights.

A tapestry woven with starlight's thread,
As forgotten phantoms rise from the dead.
In the flickering flame of the ageless glow,
Relics awaken, legends bestow.

Through moonlit woods, the glow guides near,
Where dreams take flight, casting off fear.
Together we dance, the world still spins,
In twilight's embrace, where magic begins.

Enchanted Light Above the Wyrm's Feast

Above the feast where shadows loom,
Enchanted light dispels the gloom.
With laughter echoing in the night,
Wyrm's delight, in a glorious sight.

Beneath grand arches, tales are spun,
As firelight flickers, stories run.
In the heart of revelry, spirits rise,
To the enchanted rhythms of the skies.

Upon golden bowls, the treasures gleam,
As eyes twinkle with every dream.
Around the table, magic leaps,
In the warmth of joy, the memory keeps.

With a whisper sweet, the candle's flame,
Illuminates hearts in the wyrm's name.
United in revel, a bond robust,
In every gleam lies the shared trust.

Celestial Glow in a Fiery Realm

In the heart of night, stars ignite,
Whispers of magic, glowing bright.
Fiery embers kiss the sky,
As dreams take flight, on wings they fly.

Crimson hues dance on the breeze,
While shadows flicker like restless leaves.
Within the flames, secrets reside,
Guardians of lore, where legends bide.

The moon, a lantern in darkness veiled,
Guides lost souls when hope has failed.
In a realm where fire meets the blue,
The celestial glow beckons you.

Every spark a story, untold yet bright,
Fires of passion, warm the night.
Embrace the warmth, let worries cease,
In this radiant land, find your peace.

Glinting Shadows Over the Dragon's Essence

In the depths where dragons dwell,
Tales of glory and magic swell.
Glinting shadows weave a song,
Echoes of power, ancient, strong.

Wings unfurl in twilight's embrace,
A luminous dance of grace and pace.
In the stillness, a heartbeat soars,
As myths awaken through iron doors.

Crimson scales and sapphire eyes,
A befitting tribute to the skies.
From the cavern, a storm takes flight,
Awakening dreams in the dead of night.

The essence of fire, a glorious sight,
Glinting shadows merge with the light.
Such power lies in silence deep,
As dragons guard the secrets they keep.

Ethereal Light Above the Wyrm's Grail

Above the grail where wyrms reside,
An ethereal glow, a guardian's guide.
Wisps of magic, shimmering bright,
Illuminate paths through the heart of night.

In the quiet, ancient whispers call,
Echoes of legends that never fall.
Between the stars and the moon's sweet sigh,
Magic flows like a lullaby.

Beneath the gaze of watchers high,
Dreams awaken as shadows fly.
With every pulse, the night unfolds,
A tapestry woven with tales of old.

Wyrms descend from the heavens afar,
Their breath ignites the night like a star.
In this realm, where spirits glide,
Ethereal light and magic collide.

Chasing the Luminescent Mirage

In the mist of dawn, a vision gleams,
Chasing shadows, lost in dreams.
A luminescent mirage appears,
Drawing forth both hope and fears.

Through the fields where soft winds sigh,
Magic dances, low and high.
The glimmer calls with a siren's song,
Enticing hearts to venture along.

Every step, a fleeting chase,
In the glow of this enchanted space.
Reality bends where magic flows,
In the heart of the dream, true beauty grows.

As dusk descends, the echoes fade,
Still, the mirage in memory stayed.
In every corner of life's embrace,
Chase the light, find your place.

Celestial Ripples Above Fire-Kissed Waters

Beneath the stars, the waters gleam,
Ripples dance like a whispered dream.
Flames flicker bright, a fiery embrace,
A night of wonders, a timeless grace.

Moonlight weaves through the twilight's veil,
Casting shadows where legends sail.
Whispers of magic, so soft and clear,
As fire-kissed waters draw ever near.

The nightingale sings to the silver waves,
Awakening stories from ancient graves.
In every ripple, a tale unfolds,
Of brave-hearted dreams and treasures untold.

A canvas bright where spirits play,
Carving paths of twilight gray.
In the hush of night, life sways and swirls,
As celestial ripples unfold their pearls.

Embers glow in the distance afar,
Guiding lost souls like a wishing star.
Through shadows deep, they'll chart their course,
With fire-kissed waters, a guiding force.

Twilight Reflections in the Dragon's Heart

At dusk's embrace, two worlds collide,
Mirrored skies where secrets hide.
Within the heart of scales so bright,
Twilight glimmers with magic's light.

Wings unfurl like pages turned,
Beneath the moon, the stars have yearned.
In every flicker, the past resides,
In the dragon's heart, where wisdom hides.

Mirthful laughter of the night,
Echoes weave into a hushed flight.
In stories deep, the dragons soar,
Guardians of realms forevermore.

A breath of fire ignites the skies,
Painting realms with luminous cries.
Through twilight's glow, enchantments weave,
In the dragon's heart, all believe.

As shadows dance and dreams ignite,
In dusk's embrace, all feels right.
Reflections twinkle, aglow with fate,
In the heart of legends, we contemplate.

Celestial Currents Breathe Life to Legends

In a realm where time can bend,
Celestial currents twist and wend.
Breathing life into tales long lost,
Eternal whispers, no matter the cost.

Stars collide in a cosmic play,
Painting legends with hues of gray.
Knowledge flows like a gentle stream,
Cradling dreams within a dream.

From ancient echoes, shadows rise,
Carried onward through endless skies.
Each current pulses with heart and soul,
A mystical force that makes us whole.

In the tapestry of night, they weave,
Threads of courage, we dare to believe.
Across the ages, through space and time,
Celestial currents sing their rhyme.

So let the stars guide your gaze,
In a dance of light, a wondrous haze.
For when you listen, you shall see,
Legends awaken, forever free.

Glowing Embers in the Imagined Skies

As dusk unfurls its velvet arms,
The heavens glow with ancient charms.
Embers drift on a whispered breeze,
Igniting dreams like shimmering leaves.

In whispered tales of worlds unknown,
Imagined skies where seeds are sown.
Stars awaken in opalescent hues,
Painting the night with spectral views.

Through time's doorway, the past does call,
Reflecting shadows in the night's thrall.
Embers glow with a fiery light,
Guiding the lost through endless night.

In the framework of celestial art,
Each twinkling star plays its part.
With every flicker, a wish takes flight,
In the imagined skies, hearts ignite.

So linger here, where the magic flows,
With glowing embers that love bestows.
In the tapestry of night's embrace,
Find your dreams in this timeless space.

Celestial Whispers in the Night

In velvet skies where shadows dance,
The stars alight like dreams' advance.
A hush unfolds, the night takes flight,
With whispers soft, it veils the light.

Moonbeams weave through trembling trees,
As secrets float upon the breeze.
They speak of worlds both far and near,
Of ancient tales for hearts to hear.

Each sparkling gem a story spun,
Of battles lost, of victories won.
The silence holds a magic true,
A cosmic tune that pulls anew.

In the stillness, dreams ignite,
In celestial whispers, hearts take flight.
With laughter sweet and shadows slight,
The night unfolds its pure delight.

So gaze upon the heavens high,
Let wonders rise, let spirits fly.
In every flicker, every sight,
Are celestial whispers in the night.

Luminous Shadows Beneath Mythic Beasts

Beneath the skies where dragons soar,
Luminous shadows grace the floor.
In emerald glades where legends blend,
The ancient songs of twilight mend.

With wings unfurled and hearts aglow,
Mythic beasts through moonlit glow.
They whisper low in timeless rimes,
Of ages past and bygone chimes.

Glints of gold on silver streams,
Weave through the fabric of our dreams.
Each tale of old, a spark so bright,
Ignites the flames of pure delight.

The forest breathes, a living lore,
As shadows dance forevermore.
In every rustle, every sigh,
Lies the promise of the sky.

So wander forth where wonders gleam,
In luminous shadows, let your heart dream.
For in this realm where magic meets,
Lies a truth that never retreats.

Ethereal Glow Over Fiery Vessels

Upon the waves where whispers gleam,
Ethereal glow ignites the beam.
As fiery vessels chart the night,
Their sails aflame in ghostly light.

The ocean sings with tales untold,
Of mariners fierce and hearts of gold.
Each cresting wave, a dance of fate,
In twilight's grasp, they navigate.

The stars they guide through misty seas,
Are echoes caught in balmy breeze.
With every heartbeat, every sigh,
A journey etched beneath the sky.

In turbulent tides, their spirits mix,
With every ripple, every fix.
An ethereal glow, their compass bright,
Leads them forth into the light.

So sail away on dreams that flow,
Seek shores where ethereal spirits glow.
For on this path where waters roll,
Lies the vessel's ever-questing soul.

Starlit Echoes in the Serpent's Brew

In cauldrons deep where shadows swirl,
Starlit echoes form and twirl.
The serpent sings a haunting tune,
Beneath the watchful gaze of moon.

With flickering flames and midnight's charm,
It weaves enchantments, soft and warm.
Each drop of potion tells a tale,
Of dreams and fears that softly sail.

The air grows thick with magic's kiss,
Within the brew, a chance for bliss.
As starlit glimmers dance on skin,
The heart awakens, sparks within.

From tangled roots to skies above,
The serpent sways with ancient love.
In every sip, a wish to make,
A bridge to cross, a path to take.

So linger long where wonders bloom,
In the serpent's brew, dispel the gloom.
For starlit echoes softly call,
A siren's song that enchants all.

Flickers of Magic in the Dragon's Eye

In a cavern deep, where shadows play,
Flickers of magic dance and sway.
Emerald scales in a glimmering light,
A heartbeat echoes through the night.

Ancient whispers of lore profound,
In the dragon's eye, secrets abound.
Sparkling visions of treasures untold,
A tapestry woven with threads of gold.

Wings beat softly, like a distant drum,
A promise of stories yet to come.
Embers of wonder ignite the sky,
In the flickers of magic, dreams learn to fly.

Legends entwined in a flickering dance,
Calling the brave for a chance romance.
The pulse of the past in each fiery glance,
As hearts beat fast in a daring stance.

In the hush of night, where shadows loom,
The dragon awakens from slumber's gloom.
With flickers of magic in depths of its eye,
A world vast and wondrous begins to fly.

Faerie Glow Over Mythical Morsels

Amidst the glades where faeries dwell,
Whispers of sweetness weave a spell.
Morsels of magic on petals lie,
Dew-kissed dreams beneath the sky.

Glimmers of laughter, soft and bright,
Dancing 'round under the pale moonlight.
In every nibble, a tale is spun,
Of kingdoms lost and battles won.

With twinkling eyes and wings aglow,
They offer delights from roots below.
A fluttering touch of magic's grace,
A spark of wonder in every place.

Beneath the boughs that shelter the night,
The faerie glow brings pure delight.
Mythical morsels, sweet and rare,
In twilight's embrace, they linger there.

Yet heed the warning, oh traveler dear,
For a faerie's jest can bring you near.
With faerie glow and morsels divine,
Time may bend, and fate entwine.

Nocturnal Glimmers Above Fiery Venom

In shadows thick, where secrets creep,
Nocturnal glimmers awaken from sleep.
A serpent's hiss, a flicker of flame,
Fiery venom, yet never the same.

Darkness dances, with whispers to share,
A tale of caution, lurking with care.
In the eye of the storm, where shadows weave,
Glimmers of hope, if one dares believe.

The moonlight's glow paints the eerie scene,
In phosphorescence so vibrant and keen.
A tapestry woven from danger's thread,
With tales of heroes long since dead.

Through thorns and brambles, persistence shows,
In nocturnal glimmers, the brave heart glows.
Fiery venom may threaten the night,
Yet courage ignites the path to light.

In the realm where darkness makes its home,
Daring souls find strength as they roam.
With nocturnal glimmers, they forge their way,
Through serpents' venom, come what may.

Dreamlike Luminescence in the Heart of Legends

In twilight's hush, where shadows remain,
Dreamlike luminescence calls out your name.
The heart of legends beats soft and slow,
In the echoes of stories that shine and glow.

Each flickering star, a tale to unfold,
Adventures of heroes, both brave and bold.
With whispers of magic in the evening air,
The dreams of the past are woven with care.

In the forest deep, where the wild things sing,
A tapestry woven of courage they bring.
Each heartbeat a story, each sigh a song,
Inviting the wanderers to come along.

Moonbeams sprinkle gold on the path ahead,
In dreamlike luminescence, all fears shed.
The heart of legends, a compass true,
Guides the lost souls to paths anew.

And as the night wraps the world in peace,
Dreamlike luminescence offers release.
For within every heart, a legend may lie,
Waiting for starlight to help it fly.

Shimmering Visions Above the Beast's Brow

In the mist, a creature waits,
With eyes that gleam like stars above,
A world of dreams and shadowed fates,
Whispers of magic, tales of love.

Every flicker, every spark,
Carved in silence, ancient lore,
The moonlight dances, soft and stark,
Awakening secrets from the core.

Beneath the roar, a heart beats slow,
In twilight's grasp, the truth unfurls,
A spellbound beast, with wisdom flow,
Holds the key to hidden worlds.

Through realms of light, the visions soar,
Upon the brow, the shimmer gleams,
A promise made, forevermore,
In every breath, the wildest dreams.

With every pulse, in timeless night,
The universe in balance sways,
A harmony of dark and light,
The call of magic, endless days.

Twilight Aura Over the Mythic Grail

In the hush of twilight's glow,
A chalice stands, aglow with fate,
Legends whispered, tales of woe,
The sacred quest, the heart's debate.

Through moonlit paths, the heroes tread,
With hopes entwined in shadows cast,
Each step they take, a promise spread,
To seek the grail, a dream steadfast.

Embers flicker, hearts alight,
As stars align in cosmic dance,
In this hour, the magic's bright,
To seize the chance, the wild romance.

Reflections stir in golden streams,
An aura wraps the mystical prize,
Hope glimmers soft, as hope redeems,
Unveiling hidden, wondrous skies.

In twilight's cradle, fate is swayed,
With every breath, an echo calls,
A journey forged, adventures laid,
In the embrace of destiny's walls.

Radiant Flames in a Legendary Embrace

In the heart of night, a fire burns,
With whispers loud, the legends speak,
Of battles fought, and fortune earned,
In flames that dance, as shadows peak.

A band of souls, both brave and bold,
Together bound, through trials faced,
In flickers bright, their stories told,
With fiery grace, each moment laced.

Through ash and ember, heroes rise,
Forged in the blaze of radiant heat,
In every spark, a promise lies,
An oath to stand, with fate's heartbeat.

In each embrace, the warmth reveals,
A bond unbreakable, fierce as flame,
Together they share, their fates, their seals,
In the light of destiny, none are the same.

The radiant glow of legends made,
Illuminates paths of those who dare,
In every flame, a magic laid,
To light the dark with hearts laid bare.

Strands of Light Amongst Scales and Sorrow

Amidst the depths where shadows dwell,
A creature glides with grace divine,
Its scales reflect stories to tell,
Entwined in fate, a path to shine.

In sorrow's grasp, the echoes weave,
Threads of light through darkness' fray,
With every breath, the heart believes,
In beauty lost, yet found each day.

As tides of time begin to sway,
The whispers of the past arise,
In every tear, a price to pay,
For wisdom gleaned beneath strange skies.

With strands of hope that intertwine,
A shimmering dance amid despair,
Against the odds, each scale will shine,
Unraveling threads, a cosmic air.

In timeless realms, where dreams don't die,
The blend of light in sorrow's hue,
A tapestry, a reason why,
We journey forth, forever true.

Fiery Orbs Above Shadows of the Past

In twilight's hue, they gently gleam,
The fiery orbs of a whispered dream.
Casting light on shadows cast,
Revealing tales from ages past.

With every flicker, a memory wakes,
Of secrets held in the ancient lakes.
Forgotten whispers in the night,
Bring forth ghosts in swirling flight.

The dance of flames against the dark,
Ignites the heart, ignites the spark.
Through winding paths of time we tread,
With every star, a story read.

Yet in the glow, a caution found,
For every tale holds ties unbound.
A past that lingers, fierce and bold,
In fiery orbs, the truths unfold.

With vibrant dreams urging us to see,
How shadows weave through history.
In radiant orbs, the past burns bright,
Illuminating the depths of night.

Dreaming in the Light of Dragon's Lore

In lairs of stone, where legends lie,
Dragons dance across the sky.
With scales that shimmer, fierce and grand,
They guard the tales of this ancient land.

In whispered winds, their voices sing,
Of timeless quests and noble kings.
A spark ignites in the night's embrace,
As dreams take flight in the dragon's grace.

Through emerald forests, and sapphire seas,
The echoes travel on twilight's breeze.
Upon moonlit paths, we lose our fears,
And find the magic stitched in years.

Each flicker of fire, a vow that's sworn,
In dragon's light, new hopes are born.
We journey forth, with hearts aligned,
In dreams of lore, our fates entwined.

With the dawn, their glory fades,
Yet in our hearts, their flame cascades.
For we are bound by stories wise,
In every dream, in every rise.

Sibilant Lights Above the Beast's Banquet

The sibilant lights flicker and sway,
Inviting all to the beast's grand display.
Under moon's gaze, they twinkle bright,
A banquet set in the still of night.

Beneath the stars, shadows entwine,
As creatures gather to share the wine.
With laughter echoing through the trees,
A chorus sung by the twilight breeze.

Wreathed in mystery, the night unfolds,
As ancient magic in whispers molds.
Each sip of night, a truth revealed,
The banquet's joy, a fate concealed.

In sinuous forms, the tales emerge,
With every glance, a silent surge.
For in these lights, the beasts confess,
A kinship formed in starry dress.

As they feast on dreams and hopes,
The night alights with wonder's scopes.
In swirling dance, freedom calls,
Sibilant lights, where magic falls.

Radiance in the Chasm of Tales Untold

In hidden chasms where silence sleeps,
Radiance glimmers, and the darkness weeps.
Tales untold linger in the air,
Inviting seekers with hearts laid bare.

Among the echoes where shadows play,
Whispers of legends weave and sway.
Through gnarled roots and timeless stones,
The pulse of history, felt in bones.

With each step forward, the light expands,
Revealing secrets of forgotten lands.
In the depths of night, the stories bloom,
Unfolding magic dispelling gloom.

From ancient tongues of those long gone,
Emerges wisdom like a dawn.
Guiding our hearts through paths of old,
With radiance bright, the truths unfold.

In chasms deep, where echoes thrive,
We find the tales that keep dreams alive.
A light that journeys through time's embrace,
In stories shared, we find our place.

Moonlight's Kiss on the Dragon's Table

In shadows deep, the dragons stir,
A dance of wisps in soft night's blur.
With scales aglow, they take their flight,
Beneath the kiss of silver light.

Upon the table, treasures gleam,
Whispers of magic, a timeless dream.
In moonlit eyes, secrets unfold,
Tales of bravery, once bold and old.

With every flap of mighty wings,
A symphony of ancient things.
They gather close, the wise and bold,
As warmth of night begins to hold.

In stories shared, their laughter flows,
Through twilight air, where wonder grows.
Each tale a spark, each breath a flame,
Together bound, they rise in name.

So let the night enchant your soul,
With moonlight's kiss, we've found our whole.
In dragon's realm, where dreams take flight,
A world imbued with purest light.

Aetherial Light in the Realm of Dragons

In realms where stars are born anew,
The dragons rise with skies of blue.
With aether's glow, they weave and spin,
In cosmic dance, where dreams begin.

Their wings like sails in evening's breeze,
Carrying tales of ancient trees.
Each heartbeat echoes through the night,
In harmony with starlit flight.

With eyes like lanterns, fierce and wise,
They pierce the dark and light the skies.
In every roar, a thunder's song,
A timeless tale that echoes long.

From craggy peaks to valleys low,
Their spirits soar, the winds they blow.
Within their flames, the worlds collide,
In unity, where hopes abide.

So relish in the magic spun,
For in this realm, we are all one.
In aetherial light, we find our way,
Through whispers of the night and day.

Glowing Mysteries Above the Monster's Cauldron

Beneath the moon, where shadows creep,
Lies a cauldron's brew, secrets deep.
Monsters lurk with eyes agleam,
In glowing mysteries, weaving a dream.

With every bubble, a story stirs,
Of ancient curses and whispered purrs.
A flicker in the depths unfurls,
A sorcery that spins and whirls.

Around the rim, the creatures peep,
Inspired by spells and magic steep.
Their laughter dances with the light,
In cauldron's bloom, they take their flight.

With tendrils long and claws that grasp,
They conjure wonders in a clasp.
In shimmered glades, the night unfolds,
A masquerade of tales untold.

So gather round, the brave and bold,
In glowing warmth, let stories be told.
Above the cauldron, a night divine,
Where all are bound by thread and line.

Blaze and Glow in Mythical Revelry

In twilight realms, where magic sings,
The dragons dance on fiery wings.
With laughter bright, they light the night,
In blaze and glow, a wondrous sight.

Around the fire, tales ignite,
Of ancient battles, mighty and bright.
Each ember whispers secrets past,
In echoes that forever last.

With every cheer, the stars align,
For in this revelry, all is fine.
They toast to dreams and wishes bold,
In laughter's arms, their hearts are told.

In swirling sparks, their spirits play,
Carving joy in the night's array.
Each flicker bright, a hope reclaimed,
In mythical joy, forever named.

So join the dance, let worries fade,
For within this night's grand parade,
A blaze of joy, with hearts aglow,
In mythical revelry, let love flow.

Flames of Radiance in the Serpent's Hold

In shadows deep where secrets dwell,
A serpent weaves its fiery spell.
Though darkness swirls, the embers bright,
They guide the lost with flickering light.

With scales like night and eyes ablaze,
It guards the heart of ancient maze.
A dance of flicker, a breath of heat,
A challenge waits and foes they meet.

The whispers echo, tales unfold,
Of courage found, of hearts so bold.
In every spark, a story spun,
The flame ignites, the journey begun.

The serpent coils, its patience grand,
In silken grace, it deftly stands.
With every flick of tail, a thread,
Of fate entwined, where dreams are fed.

So heed the call of radiant fire,
In the serpent's hold, seek your desire.
For in the heat, your spirit sings,
And rises high on fiery wings.

A Symphony of Stars Over the Dragon's Cup

Above the realm where dragons soar,
A symphony of stars does roar.
In harmony, they twinkle bright,
Guiding souls through endless night.

The dragon stirs, with scales so fine,
It guards the cup of ancient wine.
Each drop an echo of the sky,
Where wishes drift and dreams fly high.

In melodies of light, they weave,
A tapestry that none believe.
Yet in their glow, a promise held,
Of fortunes bright, and fears dispelled.

With every note, the heavens dance,
In vibrant hues, they spin and prance.
The dragon roars, its spirits bold,
In each cup, a tale retold.

So raise your eyes and drink it deep,
The symphony your heart shall keep.
For in the stars, you'll find a thread,
Of every dream that's ever spread.

Whimsical Glow of Enchanted Waters

In pools of glimmer where whispers play,
The enchanted waters dance and sway.
With ripples soft and laughter free,
They pull you in, come dream with me.

Beneath the surface, secrets bloom,
In depth of night, dispelling gloom.
Each wave a tale, a mythic song,
Of realms unseen, where you belong.

The glow enchants, a prism bright,
It twirls with joy, a pure delight.
From faery smiles to mermaid's song,
In every lilt, its magic throng.

So dip your toes in waters clear,
Let go of doubt, embrace no fear.
The whimsy calls, let laughter roll,
As magic weaves within your soul.

In every ripple, a tale unspun,
A journey waits just 'round the sun.
So drink it in, the glow so warm,
In enchanted waters, find your charm.

The Resplendent Potion in Celestial Arms

In celestial arms where stardust flows,
The resplendent potion gently glows.
A mix of dreams, of hopes anew,
In chalices of skies so blue.

With whispers soft, it beckons near,
A sip of courage, a dash of cheer.
The potion swirls, a vibrant sight,
Turning the dark into pure light.

With every drop, a wish is spun,
A world ignites, a life begun.
In swirling colors, fate aligns,
As stars respond to those who shine.

So grasp the cup with trembling hands,
Embrace the magic where the heart stands.
For in this blend, a universe turns,
And in your spirit, the fire burns.

Dance with the dreams, let spirits soar,
In resplendent potion, find the lore.
For every sip a journey starts,
In celestial arms, mend all hearts.

Spheres of Illumination Around the Serpent's Drink

In shadows deep, where whispers weave,
A serpent stirs, a tale to believe.
With glimmers bright, the orbs do glow,
Illuminating secrets none may know.

Around the chalice, a dance unfolds,
A flicker of magic, ancient and bold.
Bright spheres collide, in a cosmic flight,
Guarding the dreams of the endless night.

In streams of silver, fate entwines,
Through slumbering echoes of olden signs.
Each sip a journey, a timeless quest,
In the serpent's drink, find peace and rest.

With every swirl, the cosmos sings,
Of forgotten realms and celestial things.
In radiant hues, the past responds,
Spheres of illumination, magic bonds.

So heed this call, let visions soar,
For in the serpent's drink, there lies much more.
With an open heart, let your spirit take wing,
In the realm of enchantment, forever spring.

Celestial Dance Over the Ancient Vessel

Upon the tide, where spirits glide,
An ancient vessel, with secrets inside.
Dancing stars in the night's embrace,
Guide the way through time and space.

Waves of silver, reflections in flight,
Celestial bodies paint the night.
Each twirl, each leap, a story unfurls,
In the heart of the ocean, dreams become pearls.

From depths unknown, a whisper calls,
For those who listen, adventure enthralls.
Over the vessel, the skies do sigh,
With every blink, the cosmos awry.

In timeless rhythm, the heavens spin,
Inviting all to journey within.
Through ancient lore, spirits awake,
As the celestial dance begins to take.

So gather your dreams, let them ascend,
Upon the vessel where wonders blend.
In the cosmic ballet, find your place,
In the celestial dance, feel the grace.

Echoes of Light in a Dragon's Dream

In twilight's embrace, where shadows creep,
A dragon stirs from a slumber deep.
With echoes of light, its dreams ignite,
Painting the world in magic's light.

Through tangled skies, the colors blend,
A tapestry woven, where dreams ascend.
In the heart of the beast, a glimmer glows,
Of ancient wisdom, the legend flows.

With every flap, a storm appears,
Filling the night with whispers and cheers.
In vivid realms of flight and flame,
The dragon roars, and none are the same.

Through echoes of light, adventures scream,
In the heart of the night, live the dream.
With scales that shimmer, it soars so high,
In the dragon's dream, together we fly.

So close your eyes, and let it be,
For in this journey, the world is free.
In the echoes of light, let your spirit beam,
As you wander the lands of the dragon's dream.

The Glow of Legends in a Seer's Cup

In a seer's cup, where visions brew,
Legends awaken, both old and new.
With gentle ripples, the stories rise,
Unfolding dreams beneath starry skies.

Each drop a whisper, a tale to unfold,
Of heroics, of magic, of glories retold.
In the depths of the cup, the past does dance,
Inviting the brave to take a chance.

With hues of amethyst, and shades of gold,
The glow of legends, forever bold.
In threads of fate, entwined are we,
In the seer's cup, find your decree.

So sip with care, and let your heart reign,
For wisdom flows through joy and pain.
In the glow of legends, seek what is true,
In the seer's cup, magic waits for you.

Let the stories guide you, and never part,
For in every legend, lies a heart.
In the seer's cup, embrace the light,
For every magic seeks the night.

Starlit Whispers in the Celestial Chalice

In the night sky, stars twinkle bright,
Whispers of magic take flight.
Underneath the satin veil,
Dreams are born, hopes set sail.

The chalice shines with cosmic light,
Filling hearts with pure delight.
Time stands still, a wondrous pause,
Lost in the magic, without cause.

Voices drift on the softest breeze,
Echoing tales of mysteries.
Galaxies dance, each star a friend,
In this realm where dreams ascend.

Every heart's desire takes its form,
In the silence, where spirits swarm.
Beneath the cloak of shimmering night,
The celestial chalice holds us tight.

So lift your gaze, let your soul soar,
For starlit whispers unlock the door.
In the crook of night, find your grace,
In the celestial chalice, your place.

Glimmers of the Emerald Serpent

In the depths of a tangled glade,
Emerald serpents weave and braid.
Glimmers hide in shadows deep,
Ancient secrets they do keep.

With scales like jewels, they glide below,
Where softest moonlight starts to glow.
A dance of fate with every scale,
In enchanted woods, they tell a tale.

Underneath the cover of leaves,
Magic stirs and softly breathes.
In whispers soft as summer rain,
The serpent weaves sorrow and pain.

Yet in this wild, where shadows dream,
Hope flickers like a distant beam.
In the glimmers, a truth will rise,
With emerald eyes and timeless sighs.

So seek the light in every glance,
Let it guide you through the dance.
In the heart of the forest green,
Glimmers of magic can be seen.

Luminous Echoes in the Arcane Vessel

In the chamber where shadows blend,
Luminous echoes seem to bend.
Within the vessel, energy flows,
A symphony that gently grows.

Whispers of spells long forgotten,
In a world where dreams are wrought and.
Ancient powers dapple the air,
In this place, fraught with care.

Beneath the moon's soft argent glow,
Secrets thrummed, a gentle flow.
Arcane voices sing with delight,
Kindled by the ghostly light.

Every flicker tells a tale anew,
Of potions made and realms askew.
In the echoes, wisdom finds its way,
Crafting fates that softly sway.

So listen close, let knowledge seep,
For in the vessel, stillness keeps.
The luminous echoes cast a net,
Binding past and future, gently set.

The Radiance of the Mystic Brew

In a cauldron, colors swirl and spin,
The mystic brew invites within.
With every stir, the magic hums,
As ancient secrets softly come.

A potion brewed from starlit dreams,
Where nothing's ever as it seems.
Each drop tastes of forgotten lore,
Unlocking tales from long before.

The aroma lingers in the air,
Calling forth those who dare.
Sip the elixir, take a chance,
Let every heartbeat join the dance.

In every flavor, a world will grow,
A symphony in every flow.
With radiant essence, spirits rise,
In this brew, the heart complies.

So gather 'round, let laughter ring,
Together we'll weave the magic's string.
In the radiance of the night's embrace,
Find your strength, find your place.

Radiant Echoes Over Dragonkind's Abode

In twilight's grasp, the scales do gleam,
Whispers float as dreams take flight.
Beneath the stars, in silence steeped,
Dragon hearts pulse, a burning light.

Mighty wings stretch wide and free,
Over valleys steeped in lore.
A symphony of strength and grace,
Each echo sings of days of yore.

In ancient caves where shadows creep,
Treasures rare, their secrets hide.
The echoes of a world once bright,
Resound in tales of dragon pride.

Night unfolds with stories born,
In fire's glow, the past revived.
With every breath, their legends soar,
In hearts of those whom they've inspired.

From misty peaks to deep ravines,
The dragonkind's domain extends.
Their legacy, a beacon bold,
In whispers shared, the magic bends.

Luminal Tales of Ephemeral Beasts

In tangled glades where shadows dance,
Flickering lights weave tales so rare.
Ephemeral forms, like whispered dreams,
Fleeting moments, light as air.

With silvered wings, the stories glow,
Beneath the moon's soft, watchful eye.
Through dappled woods, they softly glide,
While nightingale songs weave through the sky.

Each creature holds a secret deep,
Magic wrapped in delicate threads.
A flicker here, a sparkle there,
Whispers of what the starlight spreads.

In twilight's breath, their essence swirls,
Fabled spirits born of light.
In hidden nooks, they spin their tales,
Luminal dreams take joyous flight.

As dawn approaches, they take their leave,
With gentle hearts, they bid farewell.
Yet memories spark, forever bright,
In every story, they dwell.

Shining Mysteries Beneath the Serpent's Wing

Beneath the vast and azure skies,
Lies a serpent, wise and grand.
Its shimmering scales weave riddles dark,
Guarding secrets of the land.

In a world where shadows blend and fade,
Stories coil like silken threads.
Underneath the mystic wing,
All that's lost and found spreads.

Puzzles dance in twilight's glow,
Beneath the stars, they twist and turn.
Each scale a tale of love and woe,
In every flicker, hearts still burn.

When thunder roars and the night stands still,
Listen close to the serpent's sigh.
In echoes past, mysteries whisper,
A venture grand, where legends lie.

So seek the truths beneath the wing,
With every shadow, every glint.
In the serpent's gaze, behold the world,
And uncover what dreams hint.

A Kaleidoscope of Light in Mythic Realms

In realms where magic intertwines,
Colors burst like jewels in flight.
A kaleidoscope of vivid dreams,
Awakens hearts to pure delight.

With every turn, a tale unfolds,
A vibrant dance of hues and sound.
From forest glades to mountain peaks,
In every pulse, life knows no bound.

Through shimmering rivers, it flows like thought,
Wandering whispers, soft and sweet.
Mystic creatures sway on the breeze,
Each heart a rhythm, a wondrous beat.

Painted skies with endless grace,
Echo the laughter of ancient kind.
In every flicker, every glance,
The threads of life become entwined.

So gather 'round, dear dreamers bright,
Let your spirits learn to soar.
In a kaleidoscope, find the light,
Within each color lies a lore.

Spiritual Glimmers Amidst Wyrmstone Whispers

In shadows deep, where legends sleep,
Glimmers dance by the ancient keep.
Whispers float on the dragon's breath,
Carrying tales of life and death.

Underneath the moon's soft gaze,
Secrets weave through the misty haze.
Wyrmstone glints with a silver sheen,
Echoes of what has always been.

Hearts entwined, a silent thread,
Guides the way for the fearless fled.
Through caverns vast and waters wide,
Spiritual glimmers ever guide.

With potions brewed in crystal flasks,
Dreams awakened in gentle tasks.
The call of magic, profound and true,
In every heart, it stirs anew.

As twilight dances on the lea,
Wyrmstone whispers hold the key.
In every flicker, a world unfolds,
Through tales of old, the future molds.

Ancient Fires Touched by Starry Light

Fires burn with a golden hue,
Touched by starlight's tender view.
A dance of shadows, a song of night,
Ancient echoes take to flight.

Within the hearth, past stories dwell,
Of wizards wise and magic's spell.
Cinders whisper as dreams collide,
In the warmth where hopes reside.

Phoenix wings held in the blaze,
Igniting hearts with fervent gaze.
Celestial sparks in fiery embrace,
Illuminating our endless chase.

Time flows soft in embers' glance,
Ancient fires beckon to dance.
Wisdom glimmers in coal-black night,
As spirits soar on wings of light.

With each crackle, the past ignites,
Magi's laughter fills the nights.
Ancient fires, a guiding flame,
Awakening souls with whispered name.

Eternal Luminosity in the Academy of Beasts

In halls of wonder, shadows roam,
The Academy, a mystical home.
Creatures great with wisdom keen,
Guard secrets never before seen.

Whiskers twitch and feathers gleam,
Each heartbeat sings a quiet dream.
Eternal luminescence weaves,
In the tapestry that nature leaves.

Fur and scale, a sacred pact,
In unity, where spirits act.
Mystical beings, fierce and free,
Share ancient lore with you and me.

Wings unfurl in joyous flight,
Bringing stories from day to night.
Chasing shadows 'neath luminous skies,
In the Academy, wisdom lies.

A bond unbroken, eternal truth,
The whispers echo of forgotten youth.
In harmony, the world is spun,
Beneath the gaze of the timeless sun.

Here in the heart of magic's breath,
Life weaves paths through birth and death.
Eternal luminescence, bright and bold,
In harmony with creatures old.

Ethereal Drifts Over the Chalice of Time

In twilight's hold, a chalice gleams,
Filled with echoes of ancient dreams.
Ethereal drifts, soft and light,
Whispering secrets of day and night.

Glimmers rise from the depths below,
Time flows gently in a cosmic glow.
Moments captured in fluid grace,
Transforming time in a sacred space.

Stars align in a dancer's waltz,
Crafted stories held in vaults.
Every flicker, a chance to see,
Threads of fate entwined with glee.

From past to future, transitions weave,
In the chalice, what we believe.
A tapestry spun of hope and tears,
Reflects our joys, our loss, our fears.

As ethereal drifts dance in sway,
Time reveals what words can't say.
In every heartbeat, life resumes,
Filling silence with vibrant blooms.

So raise the chalice, let spirits soar,
Through the shadows, we seek for more.
With every drift, our essence shines,
In the chalice of time, love entwines.

Celestial Sparks in the Hearth of Legends

In ancient whispers, tales intertwine,
With stars igniting the velvet night.
Where heroes tread on paths divine,
Their fates alight in celestial light.

A comet's tail across the sky,
Guides dreams concealed in silken sighs.
With every wish, the moments fly,
In the hearth, where the legends rise.

Beneath the gaze of the watching moon,
The echoes of laughter blend with lore.
In twilight's glow, a hopeful tune,
Calls forth the spirits forevermore.

As flickering shadows dance and leap,
Old stories awaken in the night.
In our hearts, the dreams we keep,
Burn bright as stars, a wondrous sight.

So gather 'round, let the embers spark,
For every tale holds a myriad of ways.
In the hearth of legends, we'll leave our mark,
As celestial sparks illuminate our days.

Illumination in the Lair of Shadows

In the lair where shadows sigh,
Whispers dance on midnight winds.
A flickering flame that seeks to fly,
Illuminates mysteries where fear rescinds.

With every shadow, secrets weave,
A tapestry of dreams confined.
In the dark, we dare believe,
Illumination whispers, tender and kind.

Beneath the cloak of starlit veils,
The brave will seek what hides below.
In heartbeats loud, the courage sails,
Through haunting echoes where shadows grow.

Though twilight's grasp is chill and stark,
A glimmer shines through cold despair.
In the dark, we find our spark,
Illumination lingers in the air.

So tread with grace through whispers damp,
Let hope be light where shadows play.
For in the depths, a glowing lamp,
Awaits to guide us on our way.

Cosmic Radiance Amidst the Fabled Flames

From cosmic heights the radiance spills,
Amidst the flames of stories bold.
In each flicker, the magic thrills,
Where fables live and dreams unfold.

With every spark, a tale ignites,
In shimmering hues of countless shades.
A dance of wonder through endless nights,
In the warmth of hearth, the darkness fades.

Among the embers, a lullaby,
Sings softly of the world unseen.
Where hopes are born and moments fly,
In cosmic whispers, our souls convene.

Through trails of fire, adventures wind,
With laughter echoing through the air.
In the night, our fates aligned,
Tales of the brave, we boldly share.

So let us gaze at the vast expanse,
With open hearts and spirited dreams.
In this warmth, we take our chance,
To chase the light and hear the screams.

Flickering Secrets of the Serpent's Chalice

In the chalice where shadows twine,
Flickering secrets stir and glide.
With every drop, the stories shine,
Beneath the surface, treasures hide.

In serpentine curves, the potion swirls,
A dance of fate in liquid grace.
The whispered secrets of ancient worlds,
Entwine with magic in this sacred space.

With every taste, a tale unfolds,
Of heroes born and kingdoms lost.
In shadows deep, the truth beholds,
The power hidden within the cost.

So take a sip with careful thought,
For knowledge comes at a price so dear.
In the serpent's depths, the lessons taught,
Shall echo forth for all to hear.

Let courage light the darkest days,
As we embrace each twist and turn.
With flickering secrets, we blaze,
In the chalice's depths, our spirits burn.

Luminescent Tales from the Ember's Edge

In the heart of night where shadows play,
Whispers of magic drift and sway.
Stars like lanterns in the velvet deep,
Guarding secrets the ancients keep.

A flicker of fire ignites the gloom,
Beneath the boughs where the wildflowers bloom.
Glimmers of fate dance in the air,
Threads of destiny, brightly rare.

Luminous stories breathe and sigh,
Cascading like sparks from the midnight sky.
Each ember a tale, each flicker a dream,
Weaving enchantments that bend the seam.

Rustling leaves sing of long-lost glories,
Echoes entwined in forgotten stories.
As dawn approaches with gentle grace,
The glow remains in this sacred place.

And in the silence that follows the light,
Magic lingers, imparting its might.
Ember's edge keeps the night sublime,
In luminescent tales beyond all time.

Glinting Ambrosia in the Shadow's Grasp

Beneath the moon's gaze, shadows entwine,
Where secrets murmur and fortunes align.
In hidden alcoves, whispers arise,
Painting the darkness with glittering sighs.

Ambrosia flows from olden springs,
The nectar of dreams, borne on gossamer wings.
Sweet flavors linger, elusive and rare,
Dancing on lips, a tender affair.

In twilight's embrace, our fates converge,
As the night unfurls, our hearts emerge.
Glistening fragments of starlit lore,
Unraveling stories that thirst for more.

The shadow's grasp holds an enigmatic feel,
Tempting the brave with its ancient seal.
Beneath the canopy, destinies flow,
Glinting ambrosia in the ebb and glow.

And with each sip, we discover anew,
A world woven bright in a darker hue.
For in the shadows, magic does thrive,
Offering wisdom and will to survive.

Illuminated Whimsy Along Dragonstone

Along Dragonstone, where the waters gleam,
Whimsy wanders on the rippling stream.
Light-hearted laughter drifts on the breeze,
A tapestry of dreams that aim to please.

The sun's gentle touch paints the skies gold,
As stories of heroes and legends unfold.
Each ripple of water, a tale comes alive,
In the light of the dawn, hopes begin to thrive.

Colorful whispers embrace the air,
Echoes of magic, a jubilant flair.
With every step, enchantments are spun,
Illuminated whimsy where spirits run.

Fish leap like wishes from the depths below,
Chasing the sunlight with radiant glow.
The flapping of wings reveals the delight,
Of the creatures of whimsy, in flight, in light.

In this vibrant realm where dreams take flight,
The heart of Dragonstone shines ever bright.
Here laughter and magic weave through the air,
Illuminated whimsy, beyond compare.

Celestial Flames Touching Mythic Waters

Celestial flames dance in the night,
With whispers of gods in their radiant light.
Like brushstrokes of fire on canvas of dark,
They mingle with wishes, igniting a spark.

Mythic waters mirror the stars above,
A tranquil embrace infused with love.
Ripples ripple with stories untold,
Soft secrets flowing like liquid gold.

The flames beckon forth the dreams long lost,
Their flickering glow, a heartwarming cost.
In the echo of time, the past finds its way,
Through celestial flames that guide the stray.

A symphony of magic as night unfolds,
Where each drop of water a mystery holds.
With every spark, a tale is ignited,
In the convergence of dreams, all united.

From the depths of the sea to the heights of the sky,
The elements dance, never asking why.
Celestial flames touch the mythic waters,
In a cosmic embrace, where magic never falters.

Shimmering Spirits in the Fiery Goblet

In shadows deep, they softly swirl,
With glimmers bright, their secrets unfurl.
They dance on edges, a flickering trace,
Of laughter and whispers, a magical grace.

Their colors blend in a swirling spark,
Each spirit a tale, igniting the dark.
A goblet awaits with its textured glow,
As dreams take flight, where no one might go.

Through trails of light, they beckon us near,
With promises held in a whispering cheer.
They twirl like leaves in the autumn wind,
In the fiery goblet, where all lives begin.

These shimmering souls, elusive and bright,
Guide weary hearts through the long, endless night.
A toast to the spirits that linger and stay,
As magic unfolds, each sip leads the way.

So raise up your chalice, let wonder ignite,
With shimmering spirits, the world feels right.
For in every drink, there's a glimpse of the past,
And a future that twinkles, forever to last.

Flashes of Myth Above the Wyrm's Heart

Above the wyrm's heart, the legends unfold,
In flashes of myth, both daring and bold.
The tales woven tight in the fabric of night,
Speak of the battles, of honor and right.

Roaring winds carry the echo of lore,
Of dragons and heroes who once fought before.
With wings spread wide, they take to the skies,
Reliving the stories where courage never dies.

A flicker of flame, a shadow so vast,
The wyrm's heart beats to a thunderous past.
Each thrum a reminder of fables long spun,
Of sorrow and triumph, of battles won.

Beneath the stars, the ancient ones gleam,
In flashes of myth, we dare to dream.
With every heartbeat, the wyrm calls us near,
To witness the magic, to cherish the fear.

In the realm of the lost, where history's moored,
Flashes of myth keep our spirits restored.
So gather the tales, let them light up the dark,
For above the wyrm's heart, we leave our mark.

A Dancer's Light Over the Dragon's Draught

In moonlit glades, where shadows unite,
A dancer's light twirls, enchanting the night.
Her feet whisper secrets to the whispering trees,
As magic swirls softly upon the soft breeze.

With each graceful step, the world comes alive,
On the dragon's draught, the dreams start to thrive.
The essence of wonder, of stories untold,
Is captured in moments more precious than gold.

Her dress weaves a spell, spun from starlight,
As she beckons the glow from the depths of the night.
In echoes of laughter, in shimmering streams,
Every twirl ignites the heart's wildest dreams.

Over the chalice, her spirit takes flight,
A dance for the ages that glimmers so bright.
For in every swirl, a memory's grace,
Is etched in the heart, a transcendent space.

The dragon watches with wise, ancient eyes,
As the dancer weaves tales beneath twilight skies.
So sip from the draught, let your worries depart,
In the dance of the night, find the song in your heart.

Glistening Mists Around the Fiery Chalice

Glistening mists in the cool evening air,
Wrap 'round the chalice, a magical flare.
With whispers of dreams and the stories we hold,
They dance in the twilight, both timid and bold.

In soft, swirling shades, reflections abound,
Of hearts intertwined, where true magic is found.
The chalice awaits, with its fire alight,
As shadows and starlight embrace the night.

Through tendrils of vapor, sweet laughter we hear,
Of moments long cherished that draw ever near.
Each sip speaks of hope, in a world so bright,
Where mists wrap the chalice, guiding our sight.

The flickers of warmth from the embers below,
Match the glistening mists in a passionate glow.
For within the embrace of the fiery pulse,
Lie dreams yet to blossom, emotions convulse.

So raise high the chalice, let spirits entwine,
In glistening mists where the stars brightly shine.
With every warm draught, we find solace and peace,
As magic surrounds us, and troubles all cease.